Find the Truth!

Everything you are about to read is true *except* for one of the sentences on this page.

Which one is **TRUE**?

T or F   Mickey Mouse was Walt Disney's first famous cartoon character.

T or F   Walt Disney was the first to use sound in a cartoon.

Find the answers in this book.

Contents

Disney's original family name was D'Isigny. It changed when his ancestors moved to the United States.

4

Walt Disney

The Man Behind the Magic

WITHDRAWN

TAMRA B. ORR

Children's Press®
An Imprint of Scholastic Inc.
New York Toronto London Auckland Sydney
Mexico City New Delhi Hong Kong
Danbury, Connecticut

Content Consultant
James Marten, PhD
Professor and Chair, History Department
Marquette University
Milwaukee, Wisconsin

Library of Congress Cataloging-in-Publication Data
Orr, Tamra.
Walt Disney : the man behind the magic / by Tamra B. Orr.
pages cm.—(A true book)
Includes bibliographical references and index.
ISBN 978-0-531-24780-8 (lib. bdg.) — ISBN 978-0-531-28466-7 (pbk.)
1. Disney, Walt, 1901–1966—Juvenile literature. 2. Animators—United States—Biography—
Juvenile literature. I. Title.
NC1766.U52D55428 2013
791.43092—dc23[B]   2013005794

Front cover: Mickey Mouse and Walt Disney
Back cover: Sleeping Beauty's Castle
at Disneyland in California

Snow White and the Seven Dwarves was Disney's first major success.

THE BIG TRUTH!

Walt Disney at War

CHAPTER 1

From a Pencil to Tar

For as long as he could remember, Walt Disney loved to draw. Growing up, he drew pictures of everything. One day, it was the pigs and cows on the farm. The next, it was trees in the forest or birds on the branches.

Walt drew a picture of a horse named Rupert, owned by his neighbor Doc Sherwood, the local doctor. Sherwood liked it so much that he paid Walt a nickel for it. It was Walt's first sale!

During his lifetime, Disney won 22 Academy Awards — more than any other person.

A New Idea

One day, young Walt looked at the outside of the house on his family's farm in Marceline, Missouri. It was so plain. He knew just what to do about it! He found a bucket full of thick black tar, which was used to waterproof barrels that stored rainwater. This would be perfect for paint. Now, all Walt needed was a brush—and a helper. He

grabbed his little sister, Ruth. It was time for some fun!

Ruth (left) was two years younger than her brother Walt (right).

8

The Disneys lived in their Marceline, Missouri, home for four years.

Ruth and Walt searched for two strong sticks. Once they found them, the brother and sister dipped them into the soft, sticky tar and painted the house with pictures. Ruth was worried that the tar would not come off. Walt told her it would wash off with some water or a strong rain. However, the tar was far too sticky to come off! Long after the family moved away, the drawings stayed on the house.

Walt spent the first years of
his life in Chicago, Illinois.

CHAPTER 2

Small Town, Big Cities

Walter Elias Disney was born to Elias and Flora Disney on December 5, 1901, in Chicago, Illinois. Walt had three big brothers named Herbert, Raymond, and Roy. In 1903, his baby sister, Ruth, was born.

Walt spent most of his life in big cities. But it was his years in Marceline, Missouri, that he loved the most.

Some of Walt's earliest memories were of the natural world around him.

Moving to Marceline

When Walt was five years old, the family moved to a farm in Marceline. They wanted a simpler life. The farm had 5 acres (2 hectares) of fruit **orchards**. Walt helped herd the farm's pigs. He made the chore fun by riding on their backs. He played with the horses. He fed chickens, climbed trees, wandered through the forest, and drew whenever he could. He visited nearby train tracks, waiting for trains to go by. Walt loved living on the farm.

Walt spent much of his free time in Marceline daydreaming underneath what he later called his "dreaming tree."

The Disney family hoped to find new opportunities in Kansas City.

Back to the City

The Disneys could not make enough money to stay. In 1910, they moved to Kansas City, Missouri. Walt's father earned money with a newspaper route. Walt helped deliver the newspapers before school. He woke at 3:30 a.m. and often fell asleep in class.

Walt kept drawing whenever possible, including at school. The local barbershop gave him free haircuts in exchange for his drawings. The pictures were put in the front window for everyone to see.

Trains were a popular form of long-distance transportation in the early 1900s.

To learn more about drawing, 14-year-old Walt enrolled in Saturday classes at the Kansas City Art Institute. The next summer, he found a job he loved. It did not involve art at all. Instead, Walt worked on a train running from Kansas City to Spiro, Oklahoma, and back. He walked up and down the aisles selling newspapers, sodas, and candy. He developed a lifelong love for trains that summer.

Chicago

In 1917, the Disneys moved once again. This time, they returned to Chicago. Walt's father had saved up enough money to become co-owner of the O-Zell Jelly Factory. Walt helped at the factory by washing jars and smashing apples. He kept drawing and took classes three times a week at the Art Institute of Chicago. Walt also learned to take photographs.

Chicago's economy and population were growing rapidly around the time the Disneys moved back there.

16

CHAPTER 3

Going to War, Making Movies

Just as Walt became a teenager, the United States entered World War I (1914–1918). By 1918, two of Walt's brothers, Ray and Roy, had already left to fight. Walt wanted to join them. He was too young to join most military branches, but he knew the American Red Cross accepted 16-year-olds as ambulance drivers. There was only one catch: his parents had to sign a permission form first.

About 65 million people fought during World War I. Four million of them were American.

On His Way

Walt's father said no, but Walt's mother, Flora, was easier to convince. Flora soon gave in and signed the form. Walt was off to war!

Walt was sent to France for a year but was never close to the battlefield. He spent most of his time drawing fake war medals on soldiers' uniforms and decorating ambulances. By the war's end, Walt went home sure of one thing: he wanted to be an artist!

American Red Cross membership included 20 million adults and 11 million junior members during World War I.

An Honorable Mention

Disney's creativity and love of drawing stayed with him his entire life. They also made a lasting impression on the world. In fact, less than two years after Disney's death in 1966, the United States Postal Authority released a commemorative stamp in his honor.

Commemorative stamps celebrate anniversaries of important Americans, historic events, and famous landmarks. Two of Disney's animators designed his stamp, which was released in a ceremony in Marceline, Missouri, in September 1968.

Many people believe Ubbe Iwerks helped Disney create Mickey Mouse.

Meeting a New Friend

Though Disney knew he wanted to be an artist, finding a job as one was not so simple. He applied to work at a Kansas City newspaper as a cartoonist, but was turned down. He spent many months drawing ads for farm supply catalogs. Then his life changed in 1920, when he met Ubbe "Ub" Iwerks. Iwerks was a shy, serious artist looking for a job. Iwerks and Disney decided to start their own business.

At first, they created ads, stationery, and one-minute films about news events. But that was not enough for Disney. He wanted to make **animated** cartoons. He read everything he could about drawing moving figures—a very new idea for the 1920s. Animation took much longer than filming actors, so early animated films were short, often less than 10 minutes long. They were also silent, like all movies of the time.

Disney (left) and Iwerks (right) discuss a film project they were working on.

Moving On

Disney and Iwerks started Laugh-O-Gram Films to produce animations and other short films. For a while, it seemed as if the business might succeed. They made shorts based on fairy tales, such as *Puss in Boots* and *Cinderella*, for a company in New York. The two men also made a movie called *Tommy Tucker's Tooth* for a dentist.

Sadly, these jobs did not earn enough money to keep the business going. Finally, it closed. What would Disney do now?

Laugh-O-Gram Films was Disney's first attempt at producing animated movies.

Disney hired Lillian Bounds as an inker, a person who traced animators' drawings onto clear sheets for filming.

Welcome to Hollywood

In 1923, Disney moved to Hollywood, California, to live near his brother Roy. The two formed Disney Brothers Studio and began making short animated movies. This time, Walt Disney succeeded! People liked his movies. He hired more artists to draw cartoon characters. One of the artists was Disney's friend Iwerks. Another was a woman named Lillian Bounds. In 1925, she and Disney were married.

The cartoon character Oswald the Lucky Rabbit gave Disney a taste of success in Hollywood.

Oswald the Lucky Rabbit

In 1926, Disney was a very happy man. His company, now called Walt Disney Studios, was doing quite well. He soon created a cartoon character called Oswald the Lucky Rabbit. People of all ages loved this bunny. Oswald was featured in more than 25 short cartoons shown in movie theaters. The rabbit had become a true movie star! Then something terrible happened.

Disney had been contracted to draw and produce the Oswald cartoons for another company. In 1928, Disney found out that the company had hired most of Disney's artists away from him. Even worse, according to the contract, that company owned the Oswald character! Suddenly, Disney had lost the rabbit and his business. What was he going to do now?

Though he did less of the animation himself as his company grew, Disney still drew, sometimes sketching ideas for new characters.

CHAPTER 4

"Disney's Folly"

Disney needed a new cartoon character. A cat? No, there were too many being drawn by other companies. A rabbit? No, not again. A mouse? Sure, why not? Disney sat down and drew a mouse. He gave it red pants and huge ears. He named it Mortimer.

When Lillian heard the name, she didn't like it. It didn't sound friendly. Try Mickey instead, she suggested. And Mickey Mouse was born.

 Disney created Mickey Mouse while on a train from New York to California.

Adding Innovations

The first two movies featuring Mickey Mouse were called *Plane Crazy* and *The Gallopin' Gaucho*. Both were very popular with moviegoers.

In 1928, Disney made another movie with Mickey. This time, he added sound. The ability to use sound in movies had only recently been invented. Disney was the first to use it with animation. *Steamboat Willie* had whistles and other sound effects. Mickey whistled and spoke, as did his girlfriend, Minnie Mouse.

Disney did the voices in Steamboat Willie himself.

28

Disney won a special Academy Award in 1932 for creating Mickey Mouse.

As time passed, Disney's company grew bigger. After adding sound to his films, he also added color. In 1932, his colorful *Flowers and Trees* won an Academy Award. In 1933, millions of young people joined the Mickey Mouse Club, sharing the **slogan**, "Mickey Mice do not swear, smoke, cheat, or lie."

Soon Donald Duck, Goofy, and Pluto were added to Disney's cartoons. Mickey also became the star of his own comic strip in many newspapers.

Few people expected audiences to pay attention to an animated movie for longer than an hour.

Snow White

Disney was thrilled with how well his business was going. Now he wanted to make a full-length animated movie, rather than a short. He would base it on the story of Snow White. People said he was crazy. No one would want to see a cartoon that long! They called the idea "Disney's folly."

It took five years and about 250,000 drawings, but in 1937, *Snow White* was finished.

The movie was a huge success. It broke all records for animated films. Clearly, "Disney's folly" had not been such a crazy idea after all.

Over the next few years, Disney made more films, including *Pinocchio* (1940), *Fantasia* (1940), *Dumbo* (1941), and *Bambi* (1942). They were not quite as successful as Snow White had been. Americans had World War II (1939–1945) on their minds and didn't have as much time or money to go to the movies.

Disney continued to look for new ways to use animation. Some movies, such as *Bambi*, starred animals instead of people.

Walt Disney at War

World War II started in Europe in 1939. The United States entered the war at the end of 1941. During the war, Disney had to stop working on his next movies, *Alice in Wonderland* and *Peter Pan*. The U.S. Army took over his studio, using some spaces for storing supplies and repairing equipment.

Meanwhile, the studio made training and propaganda films for the government. Some films helped train members of the U.S. military. In films made for the general public, Mickey, Donald, and other characters reminded people to be patriotic and support the war effort.

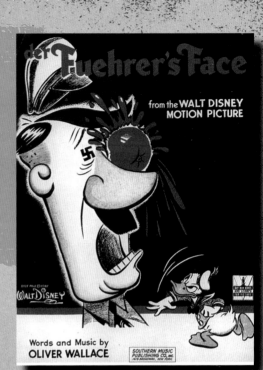

Disney often worked with government and military officials on these films. By the time the war ended in 1945, Disney Studios had produced nearly 70 hours of film for the government. One film, *Der Fuehrer's Face*, even won an Academy Award.

Disney stands with his wife and daughters Sharon (top left) and Diane (top right), not long after World War II.

CHAPTER 5

Welcome to a Happy Place

After the war, Disney Studios produced a string of hit movies, including its first live-action film, *Treasure Island*. Disney was doing well at home, too. He had a beautiful home with a movie theater, a soda fountain, and even a train and train tracks. He was also the father of two daughters, Diane and Sharon.

One day, while watching his girls ride a **carousel**, Disney had a new idea. What if he could create a park designed for families? It would have rides, food, games—and Mickey Mouse, of course!

On to Television

Disney's idea was exciting, but it was also extremely expensive. The park would cost millions of dollars. Where would he find the money?

During the 1950s, television was new and popular. Disney made a deal with the American Broadcasting Company (ABC). ABC would provide funds for his park, and Disney would allow ABC to show Disney Studios television shows. Disney created two programs: the weekly *Walt Disney's Wonderful World of Color* and the daily *Mickey Mouse Club*.

Millions of Americans started watching television regularly in the 1950s.

M-I-C, K-E-Y, M-O-U-S-E!

From 1955 to 1959, kids everywhere tuned in weekday afternoons to watch *The Mickey Mouse Club*. The show's young performers were called Mouseketeers. They always sang, "Who's the leader of the club that's made for you and me? M-I-C, K-E-Y, M-O-U-S-*E*!" From 1989 to 1996, the newly created Disney Channel played an updated version of the show. Some of those Mouseketeers became famous later. They include Ryan Gosling, Justin Timberlake, Christina Aguilera, and Britney Spears.

Walt Disney's Wonderful World of Color featured cartoons and shows. As host, Disney also spent a good part of the show talking about Disneyland, his new park under construction in Anaheim, California. People quickly became interested. Building began in 1954.

In *The Mickey Mouse Club*, young people sang, danced, and wore mouse hats with ears. Soon, those hats were being worn by children across the country. Everybody loved Mickey—and Walt Disney.

Timeline of
Walt Disney's Work

1908
Young Walt Disney sells a drawing of Rupert the horse to its owner, Doc Sherwood.

1927
Disney creates the Oswald the Lucky Rabbit cartoons.

Welcome to Disneyland!

Disneyland opened on July 17, 1955. The park covered 160 acres (65 ha) and had cost $17 million to build. There were rides, stores, and people dressed up as characters from Disney's films. It included five "lands": Main Street, Fantasyland, Adventureland, Frontierland, and Tomorrowland.

Celebrities came to the opening, which was shown live on TV. The opening was not a perfect day, however.

1954

Disney begins building his first amusement park.

1928

Disney comes up with the idea for Mickey Mouse.

The Snow White ride was just one of the activities visitors could experience at Disneyland.

Disneyland's slogan was "The happiest place on Earth."

Thousands more people showed up than were expected. It was terribly hot. Many of the water fountains did not work. Then a gas leak closed down parts of the park. Despite that, people loved Disneyland. As Disney said, "I think what I want Disneyland to be most of all is a happy place—a place where adults and children can experience together some of the wonders of life, of adventure, and feel better because of it."

Another Park

Disneyland proved so successful that it was little surprise when Disney decided to build a second park. It was to be called Walt Disney World and located in Orlando, Florida. Disney World would include a section called EPCOT, or Experimental **Prototype** Community of Tomorrow.

Disney kept making movies, naturally. During the 1950s and 1960s, he produced the animated *Sleeping Beauty*, plus the live-action films *The Shaggy Dog*, *The Absent-Minded Professor*, and *Son of Flubber*.

Disney's original plans for EPCOT had to be scaled back after construction began.

One of Disney's most popular movies, *Mary Poppins*, came out in 1964. It combined live action with animation, something few movies had done before. It won five Academy Awards.

As building plans were being finalized for Disney World, Disney's health began to suffer seriously. A lifetime smoker, he was **diagnosed** with lung cancer. Walt Disney passed away on December 15, 1966, at the age of 65.

Actors in *Mary Poppins* interacted with animated surroundings and characters.

42

Disneyland employees are called cast members.

A Lasting Legacy

After Disney's death, his brother Roy took control of the new park's construction. Disney World opened in 1971 and was a huge success.

Today, Mickey Mouse remains one of the most familiar characters in the world. Walt Disney's movies, shows, cartoons, and parks continue to bring joy and happiness to people of all ages. ★

True Statistics

Year Walt Disney was awarded the Medal of Freedom by then-president Lyndon Johnson: 1964

Number of Disneyland visitors for its grand opening: 60,000

Price of a ticket to enter Disneyland in 1955: $1.00

Price of a ticket to enter Disneyland in 2013: $81.00–87.00

Number of visitors to Disneyland between 1955 and 2010: 515 million

Size of Disney World: 29,900 acres (12,100 ha), almost twice the size of Manhattan, New York

Number of items collected by Disneyland's lost and found department each day: More than 400

Names of Mickey Mouse around the world: Topolino (Italy), Miki Kuchi (Japan), Miguel Ratoncito (Spain), Muse Pigg (Sweden), and Mikki Maus (Russia)

Did you find the truth?

Laugh·O·grams

(F) Mickey Mouse was Walt Disney's first famous cartoon character.

(T) Walt Disney was the first to use sound in a cartoon.

Resources

Books

Bodden, Valerie. *The Story of Disney*. Mankato, MN: Creative Education, 2009.

Lenburg, Jeff. *Walt Disney: The Mouse That Roared*. New York: Chelsea House Publishers, 2011.

Stewart, Whitney. *Who Was Walt Disney?* New York: Grosset & Dunlap, 2009.

Visit this Scholastic Web site for more information on Walt Disney:
★ www.factsfornow.scholastic.com
Enter the keywords **Walt Disney**

Important Words

animated (AN-uh-may-tid) — made by projecting a series of slightly different images very quickly, one right after the other, so that the characters in the images seem to move

carousel (KAR-uh-sehl) — a merry-go-round

diagnosed (dye-uhg-NOHST) — determined what is causing a health problem or illness

gaucho (GAO-choh) — a South American cowboy

orchards (OR-churdz) — areas of land where fruit or nut trees are grown

patriotic (pay-tree-AH-tik) — describing someone who has a strong loyalty to his or her country

propaganda (prah-puh-GAN-duh) — information that is spread to influence the way people think, to gain supporters, or to damage an opposing group

prototype (PROH-tuh-tipe) — the first version of an invention that tests an idea to see if it will work

slogan (SLOH-guhn) — a phrase or motto used by a business, a group, or an individual to express a goal or belief

Index

Page numbers in **bold** indicate illustrations

About the Author

Tamra Orr is the author of hundreds of books for readers of all ages. She has a degree in English and secondary education from Ball State University, in Muncie, Indiana, and now lives in the Pacific Northwest. She is the mother of four children, and loves to spend her free time reading, writing, and going camping. Raising her kids would not have been possible without Walt Disney. His movies, books, and toys could be found scattered throughout her house for many years, and she is forever indebted to the man's amazing imagination and creativity.

PHOTOGRAPHS © 2014: Alamy Images: 12 (Bill Grant), 16 (DIZ Muenchen GmbH, Sueddeutsche Zeitung Photo), 33 bottom (Everett Collection Inc), 15 (Glasshouse Images), 14 (Interfoto), 5 bottom, 24, 38 (Pictorial Press Ltd), 37 (Toddlerstock); Defense Imagery/SSgt. Walter F. Kleine: 32-33 background; Getty Images: 34 (Archive Photos), 6, 8, 10, 33 top, 41 (Hulton Archive), 40 (Time & Life Pictures); Kobal Collection/Walt Disney Pictures: 42; Newscom: 26, 39 left (1928 Disney Enterprises/ZUMAPRESS.com), 29 (Beitia Archives Digital Press Photos), 5 top, 30 (Sotheby's Agence France Presse); REX USA : cover, 43 (20th Century), 23 (Everett Collection), 9 (Richard Gardner), 3, 28 (SNAP); Shutterstock, Inc./rook76: 19; Superstock, Inc.: 36 (ClassicStock.com), back cover (Photononstop), 39 right (Steve Vidler), 13 (Universal Images Group); The Granger Collection: 18; The Image Works: 20 (Topham), 4, 25 (ullstein bild); University of Missouri-Kansas City Libraries: 21, 22, 44; Zuma Press/Disney/Entertainment Pictures: 31.